Inside you'll find 13 great walks, all
miles of Henley on Thames.

Henley is an historic market town perhaps best known for its famous Royal Regatta held each year in July. It lies between the beautiful, rolling Chiltern Hills and the tranquil River Thames. The surrounding countryside offers a wonderful choice for local walks from gentle strolls along the River Thames to slightly more demanding walks up the hills and down to the valleys. All the walks use public rights of way.

Wide range of different walks - the choice is yours!

Short or long distance walks
You'll find details of walks from the shortest of 3.5 km (2 miles) to the longest of 12 km (7.5 miles). Many of the walks are circular bringing you back to the point where you started. Several of these circular walks are located next to one another so you can simply put two or more walks together to make for a longer more challenging route. Others are linear routes where you can decide at which point you want to stop and hop onto public transport back to Henley.

Walks in the wooded hills or on the open river plain
Many of the routes take you through the undulating hills of the Chilterns Area of Outstanding Natural Beauty with its ancient woodlands, dry valleys, winding country lanes and plentiful village commons. On most of these walks you'll come across some short steep climbs. Alternatively try the relatively flat easy walking found along the River Thames and it's surrounding countryside.

Walk out then return by public transport
There are a number of linear routes which start from Henley and use lengths of well known long distance routes - the Thames Path National Trail, which runs from the river's source to the Thames Barrier, and the Oxfordshire Way, which runs from Henley to Bourton on the Water.

On the Oxfordshire Way there are several points along the route where you can make the choice to continue or follow a route to the Henley-Wallingford road (A4130) where you can catch one of the frequent running bus services back to Henley. (See Walk 12, routes A, B, C, D for more details).

On the Thames Path you can follow it from Henley to Shiplake Lock and either catch a bus, train or in the summer a boat back to Henley. (See Walk 13 for more details)

How to Get to Henley

By car
Henley is about one hour from London.
The A4130 Oxford to Maidenhead road and the A4155 Reading to Marlow road both run through the town.

By bus
There are regular bus services to Henley;

Thames Travel Tel: 01491 874216 - route X39 Henley to Oxford www.busbook.co.uk
Reading Buses Tel: 0118 9594000 - route 329 to High Wycombe
www.reading-buses.co.uk
Arriva Tel: 01494 520941 - route 329 High Wycombe, Shiplake, Dunsden Green, Reading
www.arriva.co.uk

For public transport information ring: traveline 0870 6082608

By train
Thames Trains operate an hourly service from Henley on Thames to Twyford, where connections can be made with mainline services to Oxford, Reading, Maidenhead and London (Paddington).
www.thamestrains.co.uk
National Rail Enquiries - 08457 484950 (24 hour service, local call rate).

By boat
Salter Bros Ltd run a passenger service from Reading to Henley, 7 days per week from the end of May to the beginning of September. The service consists of a daily round trip from Reading to Henley arriving at Shiplake Lock at 12.15pm (at time of writing) and leaving Henley at 4.15pm (at time of writing) to return to Reading. For further information and times please contact Salter Bros Ltd direct Tel: 0118 9572388; Website:
www.salterbros.co.uk

Further Information

Ordnance Survey Maps
The following Ordnance Survey map covers all the routes contained in this booklet:

Explorer Series (1: 25,000 or 4cm to 1km)
171 Chiltern Hills West (Henley on Thames & Wallingford)

Local attractions and accommodation
For further information on the area, on local attractions, services and accommodation please contact:

Henley Tourist Information Centre, Town Hall, Market Place, Henley on Thames, RG9 2AQ   Tel: 01491 578034

Location of Walks

Walk Details

Walk	Title	Length	Page No.	Route Options
CIRCULAR WALKS				
1	Nettlebed to Warburg Nature Reserve	6 km (3.7 miles)	12	Short cut between points 6 and 10 or between points 7 and 9. May be joined to Walk 2 for a 7.5 km (4.6 mile) route.
2	Nettlebed to Bix Bottom	6 km (3.7 miles)	14	May be joined to Walk 1 for a 7.5 km (4.6 mile) route. Start with Walk 1.
3	Bix to Middle Assendon	5 km (3.2 miles)	16	May be joined to Walk 5 for a 13 km (8 mile) route.
4	Henley to Lower Assendon	6 km (3.7 miles)	18	Short route - the walk may be halved at end of point 6, using public transport from the Fair Mile back to Henley. For a 12 km (7.5 mile) route see Walk 5. For longer linear routes using the Oxfordshire Way see Walk 12 A-D.
5	Henley, Middle Assendon, Bix & Lambridge Wood	12 km (7.5 miles)	20	Short route - the walk may be halved at the end of point 9 using public transport from Bix turn back to Henley. May be joined to Walk 6 at the end of point 15 for an alternative route back to Henley or to extend the walk. May be joined to Walk 3 to make a 13 km (8 mile) route.
6	Henley, Rotherfield Greys, Greys Court & Lambridge Wood	9 km (5.6 miles)	24	May be joined to Walk 5 for an alternative route back to Henley. May be joined to Walk 7 to create a longer more challenging route of 10.5 km (6.5 miles) - See Walk 7. A Short Cut has also been illustrated on the walk map.
7	Henley to Rotherfield Greys	8.25 km (5.2 miles)	26	May be joined to Walk 6 to a make a 10.5 km (6.5 mile) route.
8	Shiplake Row to Binfield Heath	4.5 km (3 miles)	28	May be joined with Walks 9 and or Walk 10 to make for either a 7 km (4.25 mile) or 10 km (6 mile) route.
9	Shiplake to Upper Bolney House	5 km (3.2 miles)	30	May be joined to Walk 8 and or Walk 10 to make for either a 7 km or (4.25 mile) or a 10 km (6 mile) route.
10	Lower Shiplake (Rail Station) & Thames Path	6.25 km (4 miles)	32	May be joined with Walks 8 and 9 to make for either a 10.75 km (7 mile) or 11.25 km (7 mile) walk.
11	Dunsden Green	4 km (2.5 miles)	34	This route may be split at points 3 and 6 to make two shorter walks. Simply follow Row Lane.
LINEAR ROUTES				
12	The Oxfordshire Way - 4 public transport pick up/drop off points	3.5km (2.2 miles) 5.7 km (3.5 miles) 8 km (5 miles) 9 km (5.6 miles)	36	Walk A: Henley to Lower Assendon Walk B: Henley to Middle Assendon and Bix Walk C: Henley to Bix Bottom and Nettlebed Walk D: Henley to Bix Bottom and Nettlebed
13	Thames Path National Trail	4 km (2.5 miles) 5.25 km (3.3 miles) 7 km (4.3 miles) 10.5 km (6.5 miles)	38	Henley to Lower Shiplake (Rail Station) Henley to Shiplake Lock (Summer Boat Passenger Service) Henley to Shiplake bus stop on A4155 Henley to Lower Shiplake (Rail Station) + Walk 10

Sights of Henley and Surrounds

Many of the walks pass through, by or close to some of the main highlights of Henley and its surrounds:

Warburg Nature Reserve
- owned by The Berks, Bucks & Oxon Wildlife Trust. Tel: 01491 642001(Reserve); Head Office, BBOWT, The Lodge, 1 Armstrong Road, Littlemore, Oxford, OX4 4XT. Tel: 01865 775476. Website www.wildlifetrust.org.uk/berksbucksoxon

The Trust manages over 90 nature reserves that are safe havens for rare and endangered species.

Walk 1 passes through the reserve and by the Visitors Centre where information can be obtained about the reserve and further walks available through it.

Red Kites in the Chilterns
These magnificent birds of prey with a distinctive forked tail, russet plumage and a five-foot wing span can often be seen in flight near the Warburg Nature Reserve, Bix Bottom and Middle Assendon.

In England humans persecuted red kites to extinction by the end of the 19th century. Between 1989 and 1993 red kites were reintroduced to the Chilterns from Spain, in a project now managed by English Nature and RSPB. The birds have been successfully breeding ever since. There are now over 100 pairs in the Chilterns.

The birds mainly eat carrion but also insects, earthworms and small mammals.

For further information contact the *Red Kites in the Chilterns Officer, Chilterns AONB Office, 8 Summerleys Road, Princes Risborough, Bucks HP27 9DT Tel: 01844 271306*

© RSPB Images

River & Rowing Museum
Mill Meadows, Henley RG9 1BF
Tel: 01491 415600 - for opening times and information on events and exhibitions. www.rrm.co.uk

Combines permanent exhibitions that trace the social history and ecology of the Thames, the international sport of rowing and the quest for ever faster boats, with Henley Royal Regatta and life through the ages in Henley on Thames.

Walk 13 along the Thames Path National Trail passes the Museum on route to Shiplake Lock.

Greys Court - National Trust House and Garden
Greys Court, Rotherfield Greys, Henley-on-Thames, Oxon RG9 4PG.
Tel: 01494 755564.
www.nationaltrust.org.uk

A Tudor Manor house set beside the ruins of 14th century fortifications, gardens and an unusual Tudor donkey wheel well-house can be visited.

House Open - April to end of September: Wed, Thurs & Fri 2-6 pm. Garden open April to end Sept: Tues to Sat 2-6 pm.

Walk 6 passes in front of the buildings constructed over successive centuries.

Brakspears Brewery
The Brewery, New Street, Henley on Thames
Tel: 01491 570224 for information about booking the Brewery Tour.
Website: www.brakspear.co.uk

The brewery stands close to the famous Henley bridge where it has brewed its highly acclaimed 'real Ales' since 1779.

Many Brakspears Brewery public houses can be found near or on most of the walk routes allowing you to stop for refreshments.

Thames Path National Trail
The 295 km (184 mile) Thames Path, follows England's best known river as it meanders from its source near Kemble, Gloucestershire, through tranquil water meadows, past sleepy hamlets, historic towns, castles and palaces into the City of London, finishing at the Thames Barrier at Woolwich.

Walk 13 uses a short section of the Thames Path from Henley to Shiplake Lock and Walk 10 uses the section from Shiplake Lock upstream to Shiplake College.

For further information contact: *National Trails Office, Cultural Services, Holton, Oxford OX33 1QQ. Tel: 01865 810224. Website: www.nationaltrails.gov.uk*

The Oxfordshire Way
A recreational route, 104 km (65 mile) in length from Bourton on the Water in Gloucestershire to Henley on Thames.

The route was created by the Oxfordshire Branch of the Council for the Protection of Rural England some twenty years ago. The route was chosen to link fieldpath to fieldpath right across the differing landscapes of rural Oxfordshire and has some breathtaking views. It has been adopted by Oxfordshire County Council as a regional route.

Walks 3,4,5 use sections of the Oxfordshire Way as part of the circular route. Walk 12 uses the Oxfordshire Way as part of the linear routes A, B, C, D and enables you to leave the route at 4 different points along this short section of the main route taking you to the main Henley to Wallingford road for regular bus services back to Henley.

For further information regarding the Oxfordshire Way: A Walker's Guide (£5.99) please contact: *Oxfordshire County Council, Countryside Service, Cultural Services, Holton, Oxford OX33 1QQ. Tel: 01865 810226.*
Website: www.oxfordshire.gov.uk/culture

Area of Outstanding Natural Beauty
The Chiltern Hills were designated an Area of Outstanding Natural Beauty (AONB) in 1965 and cover an area of 833 sq km (383 sq miles). The AONB extends across the counties of Oxfordshire, Buckinghamshire, Hertfordshire and Bedfordshire. It is best known for its beech woodlands, chalk downland and streams, brick and flint cottages and many fine medieval churches.
Website: www.chilternsaonb.org

The Chilterns AONB is very popular for walking with it's very dense network of public rights of way. It is crossed by two National Trails, The Ridgeway and The Thames Path, together with other recreational routes such as the Oxfordshire Way and the Chiltern Way.

Public Rights of Way

The routes described in this booklet use public rights of way. These paths and tracks allow you to explore and enjoy the depths of the countryside. Some have been used for hundreds of years, originating as routes to market, work and church. Today they are all an important part of our heritage.

Public rights of way are minor highways protected in law like all other public roads. There are 4 types:

Footpath:
A public right of way on foot only.
Waymarked by yellow arrows.

Bridleway:
A public right of way on foot, on horseback or on a bicycle. Waymarked by blue arrows.

Byway Open to All Traffic (BOAT):
A public right of way for vehicles and all other kinds of traffic, but which because of its nature is used mainly as a footpath or bridleway. Waymarked by red arrows.

Road Used as a Public Path (RUPP).
A public right of way where the public can walk and ride a horse or bicycle, but where there may also be vehicular rights. Soon to become 'restricted byways' under new legislation.

On Rights of Way you can
Take a pram, pushchair or wheelchair if the path is suitable.
Take a dog on lead or under close control
Take a short deviation around any obstruction or remove as much of it as necessary to get past.

Landowners can
Plough paths across fields - but they must be reinstated within two weeks, after which the paths must be kept free of crops and visible on the ground.
Ask you to leave land to which you have no right of access.

Oxfordshire County Council

The County Council maintains and records all the public rights of way in Oxfordshire, as well as developing recreational routes such as the Oxfordshire Way. Obstructions, dangerous animals, harassment and misleading signs on rights of way are illegal and should be reported to the County Council.

The County Council is interested in your views on this booklet and the walks described within it. Any comments or other enquiries should be addressed to:

Oxfordshire County Council, Countryside Service, Cultural Services, Holton, Oxford OX33 1QQ

Follow the Country Code:

- Enjoy the countryside and respect its life and work.
- Guard against all risk of fire.
- Fasten all gates.
- Keep your dogs under close control.
- Keep to public paths across farmland.
- Use gates and stiles to cross fences, hedges, and walls.
- Leave livestock, crops and machinery alone.
- Take your litter home.
- Help to keep all water clean.
- Protect wildlife, plants and trees.
- Take special care on country roads.
- Make no unnecessary noise.

Walk 1 Nettlebed to Warburg Nature Reserve 6 km (3.7 miles)

A pleasant walk which takes you up Windmill Hill, through woodland to Magpies before crossing a beautiful dry valley with good views of the Chiltern hills. On through the woodland of Berrick Trench before joining a level earth track which leads through the mixed woodland of the Warburg Nature Reserve to the visitor centre. Then up a fairly steep track through Soundess Wood before joining a country lane which takes you back to Nettlebed Common.

- Allow 2 hours
- 4
- 2, plus several moderate uphill sections
- Short cut between points 6 and 10 or between points 7 and 9.
  May be joined to Walk 2 to make a 7.5 km/ 4.6 mile route.
- The White Hart, Nettlebed
- Nettlebed Village Shop & Sub Post Office

- Car park near Primary School (out of school hours only), also limited parking can be found just off the Common around the Kiln area.
- Thames Travel X39 Henley (Hart Street), Wallingford, Oxford, hourly service stops at Nettlebed Kiln.
- Thames Travel 01491 874216
  www.busbook.co.uk

1 From bus stop head towards Nettlebed. Turn right down Watlington Street.

2 On the road bend turn right down Mill Road and follow bridleway straight on to gates at the end of the access track.

3 Turn left and follow white painted arrows through the trees and onto a woodland track to a house.

4 To the right of the house take the enclosed footpath (SW21) which leads onto the edge of a garden, keep straight on over a stile. Then follow tree line until you have reached the halfway point of the field, here cut diagonally across the valley to a stile on the corner of the woodland opposite. Follow well trodden path, to the right, through Berrick Trench woodland to a stile. Turn right, through gateway then cut corner of field to another stile.

5 Turn right onto a narrow earth track.

6 At bend in track, a path intersection (*short cut option*), bear right onto a track which leads you into the woodlands of Warburg Nature Reserve.

Nettlebed Kiln

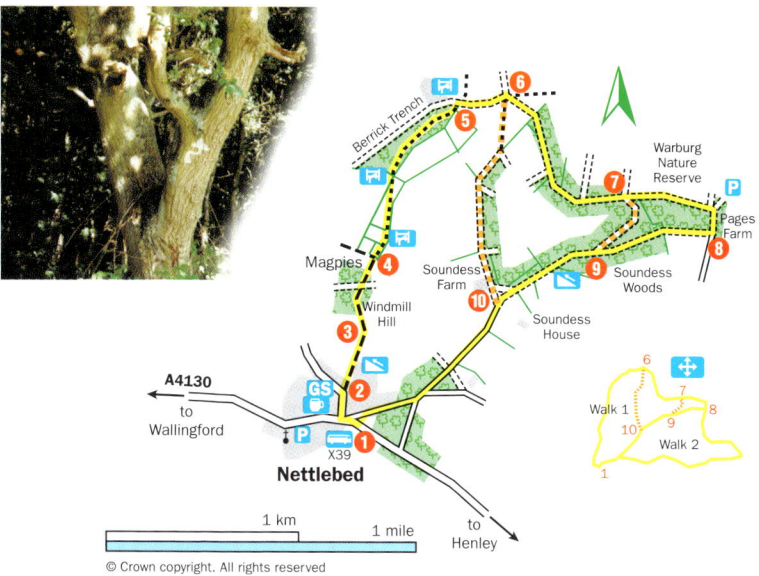

7 At track cross-road (*short cut option*) continue straight on until you reach the reserve car park. Here bear right passing the Visitor Centre onto a surfaced road. Follow the road until just passed Pages Farm. (*Route Option – join Walk 1 to Walk 2. Follow directions from Walk 2 point 5 ... follow lane for just over 1 km/0.6 miles, to the end of the walk.*)
8 Turn right onto an uphill stony track.

9 When you reach the fork in the track, bear left, up a steep hill section. Keep straight on until you meet a country lane.
10 Follow the quiet lane straight on. When it joins another lane on a bend, keep right, then right again at fork in road. This leads you back to Nettlebed and the main Wallingford/Henley road.

13

Walk 2 Nettlebed to Bix Bottom
6 km (3.7 miles)

Adjoins Walk 1 enabling you to extend route to 7.5 km (4.6 miles). The walk takes you across Nettlebed Common, along quiet country lanes before joining a track down through Soundess Wood into the Warburg Nature Reserve. You leave the Reserve on a single track lane following the picturesque valley bottom towards Bix Bottom. Red Kites may be spotted soaring above. Just after passing the ruins of St James Church you continue up a fairly steep hill, into Wellgrove Wood then on to Crocker End. Here you cross the Green before rejoining a lane back to Nettlebed Common.

- Allow 2 hours
- 2
- 1
- 1
- May be joined to Walk 1 to make a 7.5 km/ 4.6 mile route. Start with Walk 1.
- The White Hart, Nettlebed
- Nettlebed Village Store & Sub Post Office, Watlington St
- Car park near Primary School (out of school hours only), also limited parking can be found just off the Common around the Kiln area.
- Thames Travel X39 Henley (Hart Street), Wallingford, Oxford, hourly service, stops at Nettlebed Kiln.
- Thames Travel 01491 874216 www.busbook.co.uk

❶ From bus stop cross Nettlebed Common. Follow the tarmac residential lane passing the houses.
❷ At the second road junction, bear left towards 'Magpies'. At fork in road continue straight on towards Soundess House.
❸ At crossroads, by main driveway to Soundess House, continue straight on to woodland footpath track. Follow track into Warburg Nature Reserve.
❹ At the bottom of the steep section, bear right at crossroads in tracks, onto a less steep downward track and continue to end.
❺ Turn right onto single track lane and follow for just over 1 km/0.6 mile.
❻ Just beyond the hidden remains of St James Church, turn right onto an uphill footpath signposted to Crocker End. Continue on track through gateway into Wellgrove Wood. After about

St James Church

250m bear right at fork in tracks. At the next fork bear right onto a well trodden path running under an avenue of large yew trees to a stile.
❼ Cross stile and follow field edge to a stile. Continue on residential track signed to Nettlebed for about 20m, then cross a section of green, over a track to follow the left edge of the main Crocker End Green until it rejoins the lane.
❽ Follow the lane straight on, then bear right at the second road junction, back to Nettlebed Common.

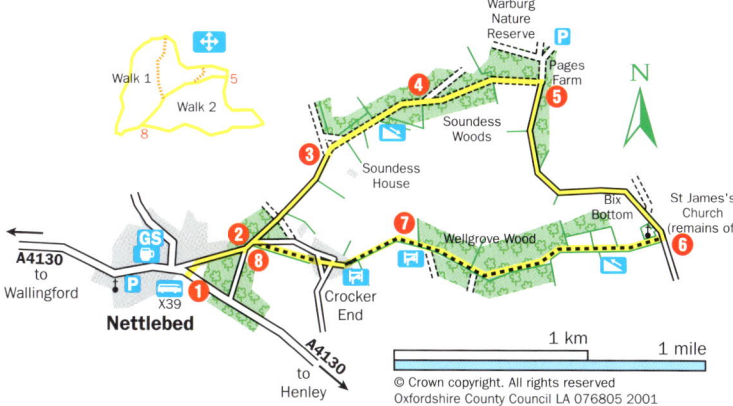

Soundess House

Walk 3 Bix to Middle Assendon
5 km (3.2 miles)

Over half this walk follows very quiet, surfaced, single track lanes. From the village of Bix the route takes you across a large open field then through Bushey Copse before passing through Valley End Farm at Bix Bottom. Here the route follows a country lane for approx 1.6 km along the picturesque valley bottom to Middle Assendon. Then you follow a footpath up a fairly steep long hill to White Lane which takes you to Bix Common and the finish.

- Allow 1½ hours
- 6
- 1 short
- 1 long
- May be joined to Walk 5 to make a 13 km/ 8 mile route.
- The Fox, Bix; The Rainbow Inn, Middle Assendon.

- Thames Travel X39 Henley (Hart Street), Wallingford, Oxford, hourly service, stops at Bix.
- Thames Travel 01491 874216 www.busbook.co.uk
- The Fox PH (A4130), also limited parking at Bix & Assendon Village Hall and next to St James Church, Bix.

❶ From the bus stop head west, on a pavement, for approx 30m (ignore first footpath on your right). Turn right onto a footpath (just by the last house before The Fox PH). Cross stile and follow left edge path which then turns into a cross field path. Continue, over bridleway (track), bearing slightly left to woodland edge.

❷ Follow footpath, marked by white arrows painted on trees, through Bushy Copse to a gate.

❸ Turn left (do not go through gate), over stile, and down short steep hill section to stile.

❹ Turn right onto an access track to Valley End Farm. Keep straight on, through gate, onto a track that runs between the farmhouse and barns (Please leave gate as you found it).

❺ Turn right onto lane and follow for 1.6 km/1 mile to Middle Assendon.

❻ Turn right at main road (B480) and continue to just passed the Rainbow Inn.

❼ At the telephone box, turn right onto a footpath, over stile, uphill crossing paddock to a stile in the right corner of the field. Here you enter an enclosed path which runs uphill (steeply in places). Turn right at top (near mast), over stile, on to White Lane.

❽ Turn left onto lane and continue to Bix Common.

❾ On bend in lane, at Common edge, follow signposted footpath across Bix Common, heading towards the left of St James Church and continue to crossroads. At crossroads turn left back to the A4130 and the bus stop.

The Rainbow Inn, Middle Assendon

The Fox Inn, Bix

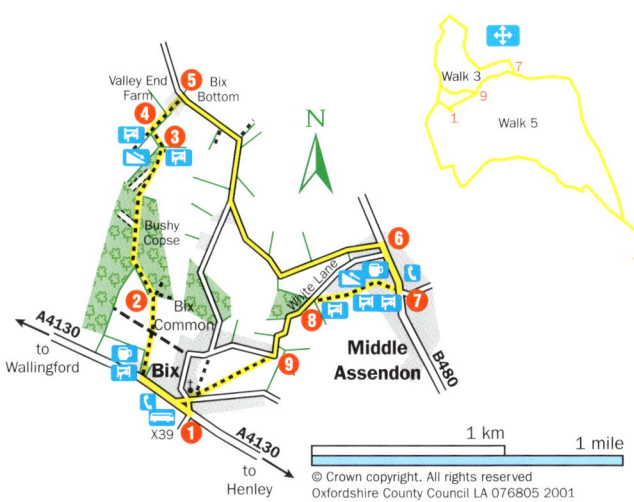

St James Church, Bix

17

Walk 4 Henley to Lower Assendon
6 km (3.7 miles)

This walk takes you along both sides of the main valley leading into Henley on Thames, locally known as the Fair Mile, and has many fine views. Part of the route uses the Oxfordshire Way recreational route which passes through what's known historically as the Deer Park of Henley Park. The route then joins a bridleway which takes you down hill through woodland, then joins a track with lovely views across the valley before reaching the village of Lower Assendon. Over the main A4130 road and up the slope of the other side of the valley. Continuing through the beech woods of Lambridge Woods which open out to some more great views before a descent to the valley bottom. Here you join the Fair Mile back to Henley on Thames.

- Allow 1¾ hours
- 0
- 2
- 2
- Short Route – the route may be halved at the end of point 6, using public transport from the Fair Mile back to Henley. For a 12 km/ 7.5 miles walk see Walk 5. For longer linear routes using the Oxfordshire Way see Walk 12 A-D.

- Henley Town centre, The Old White Horse PH, Henley; The Golden Ball, Lower Assendon
- Thames Travel X39 Henley (Hart Street), Wallingford, Oxford, hourly service. Stops on the A4130 Fair Mile, not far from the Lower Assendon turn.
- Thames Travel 01491 874216
  www.busbook.co.uk

❶ From the Henley Tourist Information Centre, walk down to traffic lights. Turn left onto Bell Street, then at roundabout take the A4130 (Northfield End). *Alternatively start at bus stop on A4130 by Fair Mile Court.*
❷ Just beyond the Old White Horse PH turn right onto the enclosed footpath marked Oxfordshire Way. Follow well trodden path up steep hill, through woodland to a kissing gate.
❸ Continue straight on passed The Mount, crossing the large field (Deer Park) between the magnificent old oak trees to another kissing gate by cow shed.
❹ Follow the field track to kissing gate opening on to a lane.
❺ Turn immediately left through a gap onto a bridleway, through woodland, then straight on to an access track down to the village of Lower Assendon.
❻ Turn left onto the main road B480 and walk 20m along the road verge. TAKE EXTRA CARE AND LOOK OUT FOR ONCOMING TRAFFIC. *(Route Option – Short Route. At (A4130) Fair Mile turn left to bus stop for services back to Henley.)*
❼ Turn right onto a path cutting the corner of the grass triangle to the Fair Mile (A4130). Cross over (WITH CARE, FAST ROAD) to the bridleway opposite.

The Old White Horse PH

8 Continue up steep hill past the cemetery. At the top of the hill cross over a farm access track.
9 Turn left at path junction marked by painted white arrows on tree, onto a bridleway (24). Follow bridleway through woods, onto the edge of the escarpment with good views across the valley. Then down hill, bearing right at fork in paths. Continue on this path to the bottom of the hill where it exits onto a residential road.
10 Turn left and at the Fair Mile (A4130) turn right and follow path back into Henley town centre.

The Golden Ball PH, Lower Assendon

19

Walk 5 Henley, Middle Assendon, Bix & Lambridge Wood
12 km (7.5 miles)

A long walk which takes in the varied and picturesque landscapes of the Chilterns. From Henley to Middle Assendon the circuit uses a section of the Oxfordshire Way recreational route which takes you through the historical Deer Park and Henley Park. The route leaves the Oxfordshire Way at Middle Assendon and joins Walk 3, taking you up to the village of Bix and around the Common. It then crosses the A4130 and before long joins Walk 6 for a short distance, then Walk 4, taking you through the large expanse of Lambridge Woods before heading down again, along the Fair Mile back to Henley town.

- Allow 3½ to 4½ hours
- 14
- 3
- 3
- Short Route – the walk may be halved at the end of point 9, using public transport from the Bix turn, where there is a bus stop. May be joined to Walk 6 at the end of point 15, for an alternative route back to Henley or to extend the walk. May be joined to Walk 3 to make a 13 km/ 8 mile route.

- Henley town centre, Old White Horse at the start of the Oxfordshire Way; The Rainbow Inn , Middle Assendon; The Fox, Bix;
- Thames Travel X39 Henley (Hart Street), Wallingford, Oxford, hourly service. Stops at Bix, Henley.
- Thames Travel 01491 874216 www.busbook.co.uk

❶ From the Henley Tourist Information Centre, walk down to traffic lights. Turn left onto Bell Street, then at roundabout take the A4130 (Northfield End). *Alternatively start at bus stop on A4130 by Fair Mile Court.*
❷ Just beyond the Old White Horse PH turn right onto the enclosed footpath, marked Oxfordshire Way. Follow well trodden path up steep hill, through woodland to a kissing gate.
❸ Continue straight on passed The Mount, crossing the large field (Deer Park) between the magnificent old oak trees to another kissing gate by cow shed. Follow the field track to kissing gate opening on to a lane.
❹ Continue straight on following the lane passing Henley Park and Tanglewood. Then follow track for approx ¾ km to the road.
❺ Cross over to footpath stile opposite and cross field diagonally left to stile. Cut field corner to stiles and cross field diagonally right down hill to woods. Follow enclosed path down to Middle Assendon. Turn left and then right, cross B480 road towards Rainbow Inn PH opposite.
❻ Join footpath, to the left of the

The Mount

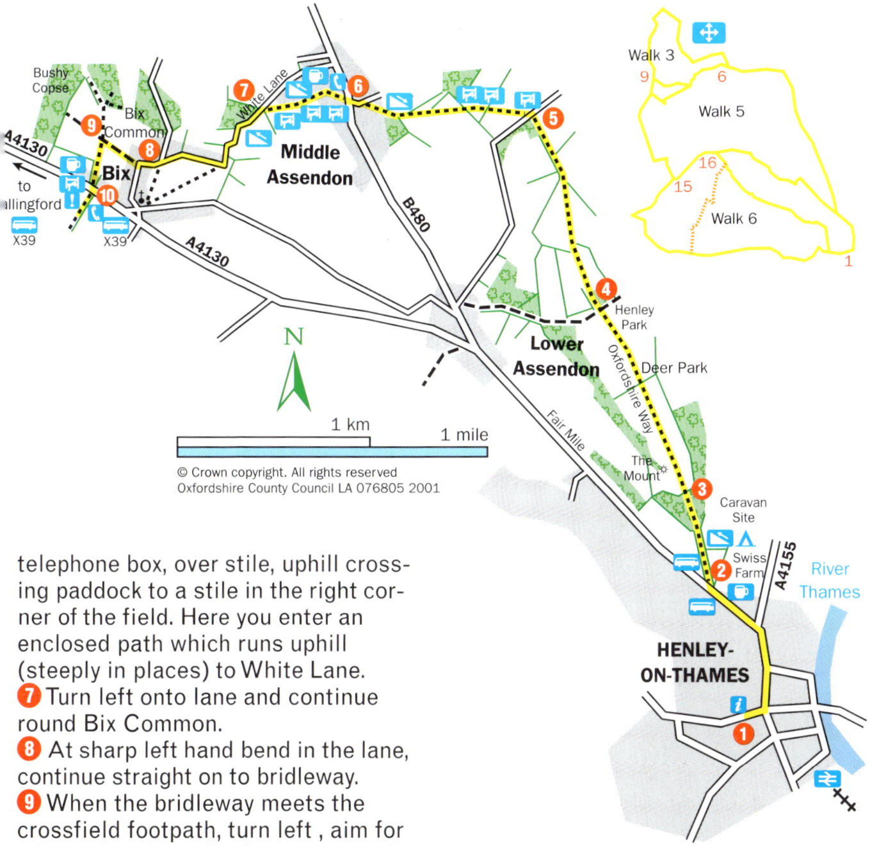

telephone box, over stile, uphill crossing paddock to a stile in the right corner of the field. Here you enter an enclosed path which runs uphill (steeply in places) to White Lane.

7 Turn left onto lane and continue round Bix Common.

8 At sharp left hand bend in the lane, continue straight on to bridleway.

9 When the bridleway meets the crossfield footpath, turn left, aim for telegraph pole with white arrow and continue to the main (A4130) road. CROSS ROAD WITH CARE to footpath to your left. (*Route Option – Short Route. Turn left to bus stop.*)

10 Follow enclosed section of path to stile. Cross over onto field edge path to another stile. Continue on field edge path, alongside the wood, to a farm track and stiles.

11 Cross track, over stile and across a small field to another two stiles. Over these and cross field towards a telegraph pole and stile.

12 Turn right to follow fenceline. When you reach the wood, cross the stile and walk straight on, ignoring stile on left just inside woodland. Continue on inside edge of woodland until you meet a wide bridleway.

13 Turn left onto bridleway and continue until you meet a cross in paths marked by white and yellow arrows on a large tree.

14 Turn right onto footpath and follow yellow painted arrows on the trees until you reach a stile on the woodland edge. Here the footpath splits, you take the footpath cross field, towards the gap and gateway in left far corner.

15 Turn left onto lane (joining Walk 6) and then at road junction cross over to left to enter Lambridge Woods (footpath signed to Lower Assendon). Follow well trodden path through woods which is marked with white painted arrows on trees (may be muddy in places during winter). (*Route Option – continue on Walk 6 point 11.*)

16 At cross in paths continue straight on. At next path junction, keep straight on joining bridleway.

17 Bear right at next path junction continuing on bridleway through woods, passing Lambridge Farm and then onto the edge of the escarpment with good views across the valley. Then down hill, bearing right at fork in paths. Continue on this path to the bottom of the hill where it exits onto a residential road.

18 Turn left and at the Fair Mile (A4130) turn right and follow path back into Henley town centre.

Lambridge Wood

View from near Lambridge Farm

Walk 6 Henley, Rotherfield Greys, Greys Court & Lambridge Wood 9 km (5.6 miles)

A scenic walk which starts with the popular bridleway called Pack and Prime Lane. The route leaves the bridleway to join an enclosed footpath which takes you into a shallow valley with rolling pastures on either side. Then through a little copse before joining a field edge route through more pasture land, later with glorious views across to Greys Court. A short stretch running parallel with a road before entering the National Trust grounds of Grey's Court, passing directly in front of the mainly Tudor Manor House. At Broadplat you enter the extensive woodlands of Lambridge Wood before emerging onto Badgemore Park Golf Course and a stroll through residential areas back to Henley.

- Allow +3 hours
- 14
- 1
- 1 steep, plus several short moderate uphill sections
- May be joined to Walk 5 for an alternative route back to Henley. Also maybe joined to Walk 7 to create a larger more challenging route 10.5 km/ 6.5 miles (See Walk 7). A short cut has been illustrated on the route map which reduces the length of the walk to 7.3 km/ 4.5 miles
- Henley town centre; The Maltsters Arms, Rotherfield Greys (short detour off main walk beyond point 6 – see route map).

❶ From Henley Town Hall (TIC), Market Place, walk up street called Gravel Hill
❷ Approx 200m beyond the entrance to Friar Park turn left onto Pack & Prime Lane (bridleway).
❸ At Henley College bear right onto enclosed track and follow downhill.
❹ At the bottom of the hill turn right, over stile, onto a footpath. Follow fenceline at valley bottom. Over stile into a copse, passing Lower Hermes on your right. Over another stile following well trodden path straight on to an access track (may be muddy in winter).
❺ Where the wood ends on your right and the track bends away up hill, keep straight on to a field access track at this point
❻ When the track bends away to the left, up hill, bear off right over a stile. Keep straight on the field edge path (*if you want to make a detour to the pub at Rotherfield Greys look out for a choice of two footpaths leading off to your left*). Continue on field edge path, over three fields passing the Old Rectory on your left. Here you have good views of Greys Court across the valley to your right. Follow the path, over a stile, onto enclosed path.
❼ Just after the enclosed section of path bends to left and up hill, bear right (before reaching lane) onto a well trodden path running parallel with a road. This path emerges onto a grass road verge for 50m.
❽ At bend in road, cross over to single track lane (left spur). After 200 m, turn right onto signed footpath which leads onto a driveway. Continue straight on passing Grey's Court.
❾ At the end of the wall, bear left onto a gravel path to stile. Continue on field edge path. After wooden bridge keep straight on, ignoring first

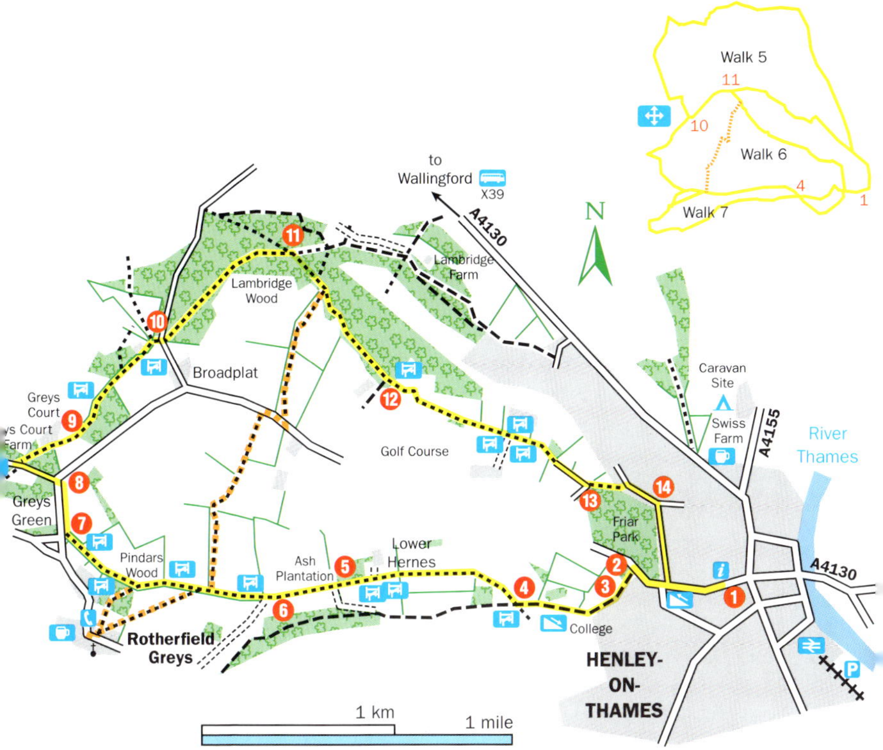

footpath leading off on your left, then left over next stile and along enclosed section to lane.

🔟 Turn right and then at road junction cross over to left to enter Lambridge Woods (footpath signed to Lower Assendon). Follow well trodden path through woods which is marked with painted arrows on trees (may be muddy in places during winter). (*Route Option – continue on Walk 5 point 16.*)

⓫ The path bends to the right and then at cross in paths turn right. At next 3 junctions keep straight on following close to the edge of the wood. Eventually the wood thins and emerges onto a golf course.

⓬ Continue straight on, up hill, diverting left for a short distance to avoid the 13th tee. Then join the pathway before leaving the golf course over a stile onto a residential access road. Over stile into Lambridge Lane.

⓭ At sharp right hand bend turn left onto an enclosed footpath which comes out onto Crisp Road.

⓯ Turn right and then at road junction turn right into Hop Gardens and follow to end of street. Turn left, either down West Street or Gravel Hill back to Market Place.

Entrance to Friar Park

Walk 7 Henley to Rotherfield Greys
8.25 km (5.2 miles)

This route may be joined to Walk 6 to make for a longer walk. This walk uses the entire length of the popular Pack & Prime bridleway (which can be very wet and muddy, especially in winter months, therefore requiring stout footwear). It then crosses a large arable field before joining the single track Dog Lane. After a short distance on another enclosed bridleway the route follows a footpath across a couple of fields to Rotherfield Greys. From the village you take a picturesque down hill route to the valley path below with rolling pastures rising from it. Along the valley before passing the playing fields of Henley College and onto residential paths back to Henley town.

- Allow +3 hours
- 13
- 2
- 2, plus 1 long moderate
- May be joined with Walk 6 to make for a 10.5 km/ 6.5 miles route

- Pubs: Henley Town Centre; The Maltsters Arms, Rotherfield Greys
- GS Henley Town Centre

❶ From Henley Town Hall (TIC), Market Place, walk up the street called Gravel Hill
❷ Approx 200 m beyond the entrance to Friar Park turn left onto Pack & Prime Lane (bridleway).
❸ At Henley College bear right onto enclosed track (bridleway). Follow it downhill and then up a long moderate hill for about a ¾ km. At cross in tracks, keep straight on into woodland. Continue until you reach the road.
❹ Cross over to footpath stile directly opposite. Cross field diagonally heading to stile between the house and hedge. Cross paddock to stile in right hand field corner.
❺ Turn left onto Dog Lane.
❻ When the lane bends sharply to the left, turn right through a bridle-gate onto an enclosed track (can be muddy in winter).
❼ After approx 25m, turn right over stile. Cut across corner of field to another stile, then cross field towards the St Nicholas Church of Rotherfield Greys. Over stile onto enclosed path running past church yard to road.
❽ Turn right and cross to footpath situated just behind the commemorative bus stop (1897 Queen Victoria's Diamond Jubilee). The footpath bears rights and follows the avenue of trees, then

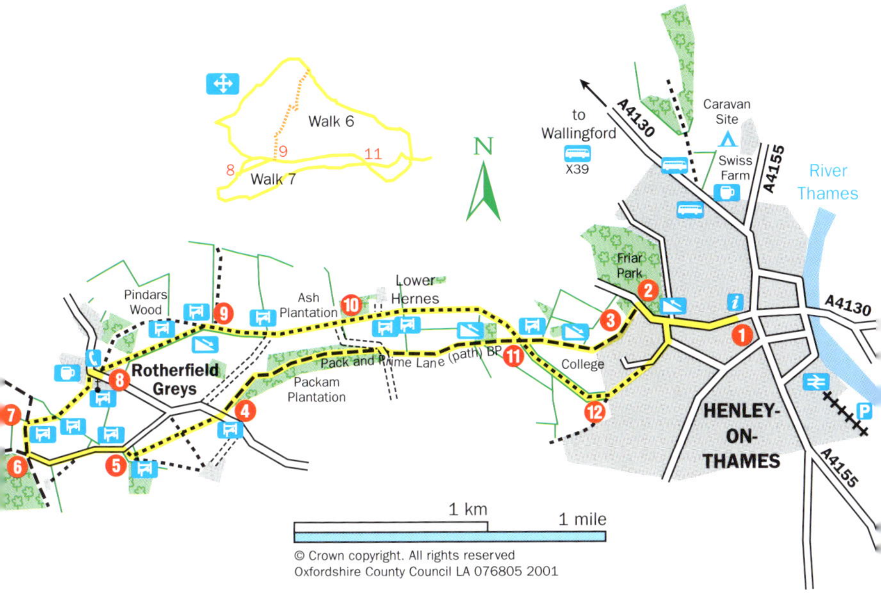

straight on down field edge path with wonderful views. At the bottom, over stile, then dog-leg right for 30m then left over another stile in hedge. (*Route Option – to join Walk 6 turn left here and follow field edge path passing the Old Rectory on your left. See Walk 6 point 6 onwards for the rest of the directions.*)

9 Turn right and follow field edge path across two fields to a stile. Keep straight on access track.

10 At junction of access tracks keep straight on, passing Ash Plantation on your left. As the track begins to bend away to the left, keep straight on, following the fenceline to a stile. Straight on through copse to stile then follow enclosed path at valley bottom to another stile.

11 Cross bridleway to stile opposite and follow enclosed path, passing Henley College playing fields on your left.

12 At kissing gate continue straight on, across residential road to a surfaced footpath opposite. Where tarmac path bears left, carry straight on, onto gravel path, with residential area on right. This path emerges onto a residential road (Paradise Road). Straight on to road junction where you turn left onto Deanfield Road back to the main road (B481). Turn right and follow Gravel Hill road back to Henley town centre.

St Nicholas Church, Rotherfield Greys

Walk 8   Shiplake Row to Binfield Heath   4.5 km (3 miles)

An easy, fairly flat walk, looping around the villages of Shiplake Row and Binfield Heath. To the south of the villages the route crosses many fields with a little section of woodland. The walk then follows a surfaced road before joining Kiln Lane which returns you to the start.

- Allow 1½ hours
- 3
- 1 moderate
- 1 moderate
- May be joined with Walks 9 and/or Walk 10 to make either a 7 km/ 4.25 mile or 10 km/ 6 mile walk
- The White Hart PH, Shiplake Row

- Post Office stores, Binfield Heath.
- Along Memorial Avenue
- Arriva/Reading Buses Route 329 (hourly service)
- Tel: 01494 520941 / 0118 9594000
  www.reading-buses.co.uk
  www.arriva.co.uk

❶ From the bus stop near Memorial Avenue, Shiplake, follow road verge south east. After approx 150m turn right onto a concrete farm track to Shiplake Court Farm. At the tight left hand bend, carry straight on, up the field, over the rise to a stile. Over stile and turn immediate right. Follow field edge for approx 200m. Cross field boundary and turn left. Follow well trodden path for approx 300m.
❷ Bear right to cross field to old access track. Straight over, following well used path to a stile by Shiplake Copse. Continue to follow fenceline through copse to another stile. Straight on following field edge to a metal kissing gate. Continue on field edge path to the road.
❸ Turn right and follow road verge for ½ km (TAKE CARE AND LOOK OUT FOR ONCOMING TRAFFIC)
❹ Opposite Fosters Lane, cross over to recreation ground and walk to far right hand corner.
❺ Cross road and small bridge to right of way opposite. Then turn right onto track known as Kiln Lane. (*Route Option – you may extend this walk at this point by joining Walk 8 with Walk 9, continuing with directions for Walk 9, starting from point 3 to end.*)
❻ Continue on Kiln Lane, passing houses and woodland, for approx 1 km (*Route Option – you may extend Walk 8 at this point by joining it with Walk 10, continuing with directions for Walk 10, starting from point 6,*

Shiplake Copse

turning left at steep bend on to a footpath to woods, and continuing to the end of point 5). Then follow lane round a sharp right hand bend back to the road where you started.

The White Hart PH

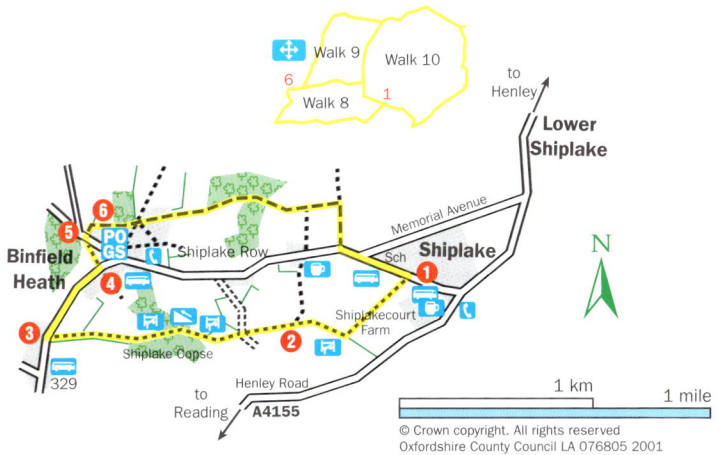

Shiplake Copse

Walk 9 Shiplake to Upper Bolney House 5 km (3.2 miles)

The north/south sections of this route take you through a mixture of fields and pockets of woodland, whilst the west/east sections use surfaced single track lanes.

- Allow 1½ hours
- 5
- 2 short steep
- 2 moderate
- May be joined to Walk 8 and/or Walk 10 to make for either a 7 km/ 4.25 mile or a 10 km/ 6 mile walk
- The White Hart, Shiplake Row;
- Post Office stores, Binfield Heath

- Along Memorial Avenue
- Arriva/Reading Buses Route 329 (hourly service)
- Tel: 01494 520941 / 0118 9594000
  www.reading-buses.co.uk
  www.arriva.co.uk
- Shiplake Station, Thames Trains
- Tel 08457 484950
  www.thamestrains.co.uk

❶ (*Alternative start - to join Walk 9 to Walk 8, start with directions for Walk 8, rejoining Walk 9 at point 3*). Start from the bus stop near Memorial Avenue, Shiplake, follow road verge north west to a track on the right (Kiln Lane). TAKE CARE ALONG ROAD VERGE, WATCHING FOR ONCOMING TRAFFIC.

Upper Hailey Wood

❷ Follow Kiln Lane, round steep left hand bend and on for approx a further kilometre (0.6 miles) to Pond House.
❸ Turn right onto a footpath leading between houses to a stile. Cross field to a gap in the corner of the field,
❹ Follow field edge path down hill to a copse. Over stile and uphill to another stile. Straight on, cross field to a stile leading into High Wood.
❺ Follow path through wood marked by white arrows painted onto trees.
❻ Emerge onto a track. Follow surfaced track straight on ignoring footpath leading off to the left on the bend. Pass Upper Bolney House and continue for another ½ km to the white gates of Little Spinneys.
(*Route option - to extend the walk by joining Walk 9 to Walk 10, continue on track to Woodlands Road and then use directions for Walk 10, starting from point 8, continue to point 6.*)
❼ Turn right, through gap and cross field, towards right corner of wood, to a stile. Continue on well trodden path through Upper Hailey Wood emerging onto a grassy track along a hedge.
❽ Rejoin Kiln Lane and follow road. Turn left back to start.

Binfield Heath stile between houses

1 km 1 mile

© Crown copyright. All rights reserved
Oxfordshire County Council LA 076805 2001

31

Walk 10 Lower Shiplake (Rail Station) and Thames Path
6.25 km (4 miles)

A varied walk taking you through residential areas of Lower Shiplake on the Thames Path National Trail before joining the picturesque River Thames towpath. You then leave the Thames Path, just passed the grounds of Shiplake College, up a steep slope to the Church of St Peter and St Paul. On through the residential areas of Shiplake to Kiln Lane. Leaving this lane to a peaceful area of woodland, across a field to a surfaced bridleway which takes you through more residential areas to the A4155 and then back to the station.

- Allow 2½ hours
- 4
- 2 moderate
- 1 steep, 1 moderate
- May be joined with Walks 8 and 9 to make for either a 10.75 km/ 7 mile or 11.25 km/ 7 mile circular walk.
- Baskerville Arms, Lower Shiplake; Plowden Arms, Shiplake; The White Hart, Shiplake Row.

- In residential area near Rail Station
- Arriva/Reading Buses Route 329 (hourly service)
- Tel: 01494 520941 / 0118 9594000
  www.reading-buses.co.uk
  www.arriva.co.uk
- Shiplake Station, Thames Trains
- Tel: 08457 484950
  www.thamestrains.co.uk

1 From Shiplake Station walk south west along Station Road for a short distance (*alternatively start from point 6, at the bus stop near Memorial Avenue - also start point for walks 8 & 9*). At the Baskerville Arms PH turn left onto Mill Road. Continue along this road for ¾ km to the Lashbrook Nursing Home.
2 Turn left onto driveway and then follow signed Thames Path to Shiplake Lock. Continue to follow Thames Path along the River Thames to beyond the boathouses of Shiplake College.
3 Just beyond the old quarry turn right onto a bridleway which leads up a steep hill to the main entrance of Shiplake College.
4 Bear left onto Church Lane passing the Church of St Peter and St Paul on your right, continue to the road.
5 Dog-leg left and then right, to road opposite, with the Plowden Arms on the corner. Continue on this road for ½ km (*Route Option – along this stretch you can join Walk 8 by turning left onto a concrete farm track to Shiplake Court Farm then follow directions for Walk 8*), when the pavement finishes walk with EXTRA CARE ALONG THE ROAD VERGE, WATCHING FOR ONCOMING TRAFFIC FOR 30m to lane on your right.
6 (*Route Option – you can join Walk 9 at this point, follow directions for Walk 9, from point 2*) Turn right onto Kiln Lane and follow to steep bend. Here continue straight on to footpath and follow through the woods on a well trodden route to a stile.
7 Cross field, heading for the right hand corner to a surfaced bridleway.
8 Turn right and follow to Woodlands Road. Cross over to bridleway opposite (Little Beeches) and follow down hill to the A4155 road.

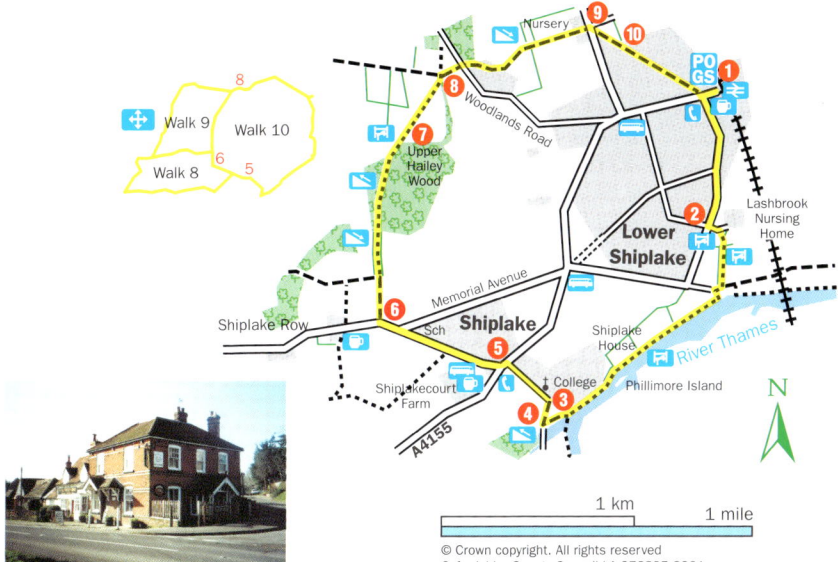

Plowden Arms, Shiplake

9 Cross main road WITH CARE to path opposite. Continue along enclosed path between paddocks to a kissing gate.
10 Follow Northfield Ave (bridleway) to Station Road (and turn left back to the station).

Shiplake College boat house

Walk 11 Dunsden Green
4 km (2.5 miles)

Situated about 7 km from Henley Town Centre and on the outskirts of Caversham, Dunsden Green is a small pretty village with quiet country lanes and scattered farms, houses and a pretty church. This walk uses the little used lanes, together with the local bridleways and one footpath. May be wet in places during the winter months especially through Blackhouse Wood and along Tagg Lane (bridleway).

- Allow 1½ hours
- 2
- No steep sections.
- The route may be split at points 3 and 6 to make two shorter walks. Simply follow Row Lane.

- The Crown & Shoulder of Mutton, Play Hatch
- Arriva/Reading Buses Route 329 (hourly service)
- Tel: 01494 520941 / 0118 9594000
  www.reading-buses.co.uk
  www.arriva.co.uk

❶ From the bus stop follow path running alongside village green for about 100m.
❷ Turn left onto bridleway signposted Littlestead Green continue to end.
❸ Turn left onto single track lane and follow bend round to the right passing Littlestead Green Farm. Beyond the farm the surface deteriorates and can be muddy and wet in winter in the woods.
❹ At the fork in tracks, keep right and continue passed reservoir to the road.
❺ Turn right and walk on verge WITH CARE for 50m. Opposite Bryants Farm turn right over stile onto a footpath. Cross field to stile, heading towards church.
❻ Turn right onto road verge and then left at bend, passing All Saints Church.
❼ At bend in road, turn sharp left, passing Glebe House. Continue on track to Crumplehorn Barn.
❽ At road junction, follow lane round to the right onto Sandpit Lane, passing The White House. Then follow track round the bend, ignoring two footpaths that spur off at this point.
❾ Leave single track lane and take the bridleway to the right of Spring Cottage. This section can be very muddy especially in winter.
❿ Bear left at fork in tracks at Chapman's Farm onto a gravel track, back to Dunsden village green.

Dunsden Green

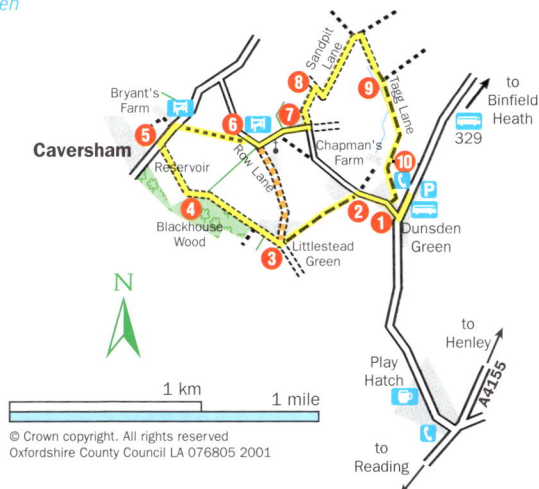

Row Lane

35

Walk 12 The Oxfordshire Way (section from Henley to Bix Bottom)

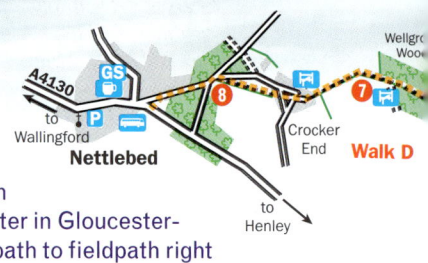

The Oxfordshire Way is a recreational route that was created by the Oxfordshire Branch of the Council for the Protection of Rural England some twenty years ago. In its entirety the walk is about 65 miles long and runs from Henley on Thames to Bourton on the Water in Gloucestershire. The route was chosen to link fieldpath to fieldpath right across the county and has some breathtaking views.

This small section of the route is easy to follow and gives you a taste of how the Oxfordshire Way continues across the differing and picturesque landscapes of the county. You may leave the Oxfordshire Way at 4 different points along this section of the route, Lower Assendon, Middle Assendon and two points at Bix Bottom. Then simply follow walk directions as detailed for that point back to bus stops on the main A4130 road that have regular bus services back to Henley town centre.

Walk	Distance	🕐	🚌	◣	◣	☕
A	3.5km/2.2 miles	1hr	0	1 uphill	1 downhill	Old White Horse (Henley), Golden Ball (L. Assendon)
B	5.7km/3.5 miles	2 hrs	5	3 uphill	1 downhill	Old White Horse (Henley), The Rainbow (Middle Assendon), The Fox (Bix)
C	8km/5 miles	3 hrs	4	2 uphill	1 downhill	Old White Horse (Henley), The Rainbow (Middle Assendon), The Fox (Bix)
D	9km/5.5 miles	+3 hrs	5	2 uphill	1 downhill	Old White Horse (Henley), The Rainbow (Middle Assendon), The White Hart (Nettlebed)

🚌 Thames Travel X39 Henley (Hart Street), Wallingford, Oxford, hourly service, stops at Fair Mile, Bix and Nettlebed 📞 Thames Travel 01491 874216 www.busbook.co.uk

ALL FOUR WALKS START FROM THIS POINT
Decide at which point you wish to leave and then follow the directions back to the A4130 as detailed.

❶ From Henley Tourist Information Centre, walk down to traffic lights. Turn left onto Bell Street, then at roundabout take the A4130 (Northfield End). *Alternatively start at bus stop on A4130 by Fair Mile Court.*
❷ Just beyond the Old White Horse PH turn right onto the footpath signed Oxfordshire Way. Follow well trodden, enclosed path uphill, through woodland to kissing gate.
❸ Continue straight on passed The Mount, crossing the large field (Deer Park) between the magnificent old oak trees to another kissing gate by cow shed. Follow the field track to the lane.

WALK A
Leave the Oxfordshire Way at this point and follow walk directions points 5, to the end of 6, detailed in Walk 4 Henley

to Lower Assendon.
Once you have reached the main A4130 road bear left and you will find a bus stop on the Fair Mile for buses back to Henley. Alternatively simply continue walking along the Fair Mile back to Henley.

4 Continue straight on following the lane

WALK C
Leave the Oxfordshire Way at this point. Turn left onto a footpath which leads you between the farmhouse and barns of Valley End Farm. Continue through gate onto field edge track. Turn left after approx 100m, over a stile onto a field edge footpath leading a short steep up hill section to a stile. Turn right and follow track through woods marked by painted arrows on trees, ignoring the other tracks. After almost a kilometre the path emerges from the woods. Head straight on towards the field opposite, leading between two fences to a stile to the A4130 road Turn left to find a bus stop for services back to Henley.

7 Continue on lane to the remains of St James Church.

passed Henley Park. Then follow track for approx ¾ km to the road

5 Cross over to footpath opposite and cross field diagonally left to stile. Cut field corner to stiles and cross field diagonally right down hill to woods. Follow enclosed path down to Middle Assendon. Turn left and then right. Cross B480 road towards Rainbow Inn PH opposite

WALK B
Leave the Oxfordshire Way at this point and follow directions, points 7, 8, 9, 10 detailed in Walk 3: Bix to Middle Assendon.
Once you have reached the main A4130 you will find a bus stop to your right for buses back to Henley.

6 Turn right and follow B480 for approx 100m. Ignore White Lane but turn up lane just beyond to Bix Bottom. Follow lane to Bix Bottom, Valley End Farm.

WALK D
Leave the Oxfordshire Way at this point and follow directions, points 6, 7, and 8 detailed in Walk 2: Nettlebed to Bix Bottom. You will find the bus stop just beyond Nettlebed Common for regular services back to Henley.

37

Walk 13 The Thames Path National Trail

The Thames Path was opened as a National Trail in 1996. It follows the River Thames for approximately 184 miles, from its source near Cirencester through water meadows, historic towns and villages to the heart of London; finishing at the Thames Barrier. The route is marked by recognisable Thames Path National Trail signposts and waymarks along its entire length.

The section of the Thames Path described in this guide offers easy going and level walking. It also has a variety of riverside attractions such as The River & Rowing Museum at Henley, the long wooden causeway leading to Marsh Lock and the beautiful water meadows down near Shiplake Lock, plus the opportunity in the summer to use the Salter's passenger boat service for one leg of your walk.

There are several options available for walking this short section of the Thames Path. For example you may choose to walk as far as Shiplake Station and return to Henley by train. Alternatively you may wish to use the daily summer passenger boat service offered by Salter's boats and therefore walk in the morning from Henley to Shiplake Lock to return in the afternoon to Henley by boat (please check departure times prior to starting your walk, see front of guide for more details). There are also several bus stops (hourly service) not far from the Thames Path which provide you with several options as to where you wish to stop and return to Henley (see walk map for location of bus stops). Lastly you may wish to join the Thames Path walk to circular Walk 10 which extends the walk to 10.5 km/6.5 miles and returns you to Shiplake Station.

Henley to Shiplake Rail Station
4 km (2.5 miles)

From Henley Tourist Information Centre, walk down to the traffic lights, straight on Hart St, to just beyond St Marys's church. Turn right, Thames Side, at the traffic lights by The Angel pub, and follow the tarmac path along the bank of the river, passing Hobbs & Sons boats. Further up the towpath by Mill Meadows park is the landing stage of Salters Boats. (*If you wish to visit the River & Rowing Museum, this is situated towards the end of the park on the far side.*)

After a short enclosed section leading to the end of Mill Lane, follow the signpost, directing the Thames Path onto a wooden causeway to Marsh Lock and back onto a causeway to the river bank.

Follow the field edge, river bank path round to a footbridge. Continue on the waymarked enclosed section leading past Fairacres and it's miniature railway and rail station.

Straight on to a residential road and follow for just over ½ km before following the signs that direct you right, onto an enclosed path. This emerges onto a residential road. Here turn right to Shiplake Railway Station and level crossing.

Shiplake Rail Station to Shiplake Lock
Distance from Henley 5.25 km (3.3 miles)

(*Route Option – this is the point where the Thames Path walk joins circular Walk 10 (6.25 km /4 miles) which returns you to Shiplake Station*)

From Shiplake Station walk south west along Station Road for a short distance. At the Baskerville Arms PH, turn left onto Mill Road. Continue along this road for 0.75 km to the turning for Lashbrook Nursing Home.

Turn left onto driveway and then follow signed Thames Path down steps to stile. Cut field corner diagonally to another stile, then follow field edge to Mill Lane. Turn right and then left towards Shiplake Lock. (*If you wish to use the summer Salter's Boats daily passenger service to return to Henley, you will find the landing stage for the boat at Shiplake Lock.*)

Shiplake Lock to bus stop on A4155
Distance from Henley 7 km (4.3 miles)

Just before the lock turn right through a kissing gate and follow the river bank. Continue to follow the Thames Path to beyond the boathouses of Shiplake College.

Just beyond the old quarry (on your right), turn right onto a bridleway which leads up a steep hill to the main entrance of Shiplake College.

Bear left onto Church Lane, passing the Church of St Peter and St Paul on your right, continue to the road (A4155). Dog-leg left and then right, to road opposite, with the Plowden Arms on the corner. Just beyond the pub you will find the bus stop.

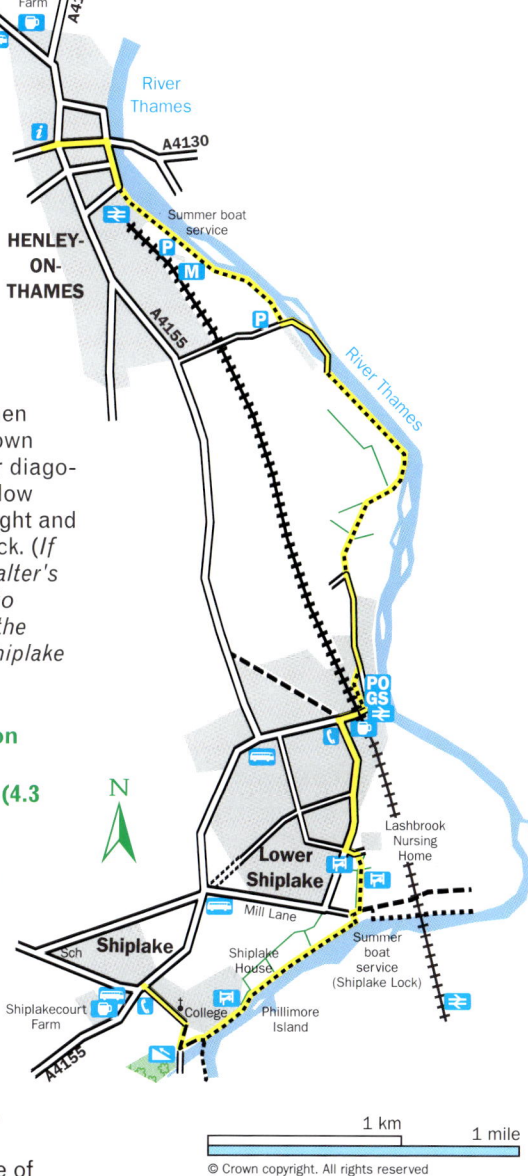

Notes